Grammar Gremlins

Don K. Ferguson

Glenbridge Publishing Ltd.

Book Illustrations

Patricia Hobbs

Library of Congress Catalog Card Number: LC 94-79511

International Standard Book Number: 0-944435-32-7

Printed in U. S. A.

Dedicated to Barbara, my beloved wife of 40 years, who is always enthusiastic about any project I undertake and who suggested that I write this book.

ACKNOWLEDGMENTS

Grateful acknowledgment is made to the following publishers, from whose works excerpts are quoted herein:

Addison-Wesley Publishing Company:

The Associated Press Stylebook and Libel Manual. Copyright 1992 by The Associated Press. By permission.

Advertising Age:

Howard G. (Scotty) Sawyer, "Loose Talk; A War to Save Language." *Advertising Age,* 1991. By permission.

Beacon Press:

Rosalie Maggio, *The Bias-Free Word Finder.* Copyright 1991 by Beacon Press. By permission.

Glencoe Division of Macmillan/McGraw-Hill Publishing Company:

The Gregg Reference Manual, Seventh Edition. Copyright 1992 by Glencoe Division of Macmillan/McGraw Hill School Publishing Company.

Harcourt Brace College Publishers:

Hodges' Harbrace College Handbook, Twelfth Edition. Copyright 1994 by Harcourt Brace & Company.

Houghton Mifflin Company:

The American Heritage Dictionary of the English Language, Third Edition. Copyright 1992 by Houghton Mifflin Company. By permission.

Merriam-Webster Inc., Publishers:

Webster's Dictionary of English Usage. Copyright 1989 by Merriam-Webster Inc. By permission.

Webster's Ninth New Collegiate Dictionary. Copyright 1991 by Merriam-Webster Inc. By permission.

Webster's New International Dictionary of the English Language. Copyright 1913 by G. & C. Merriam Co. By permission.

Oxford University Press:

The Oxford English Dictionary. Copyright 1992 by Oxford University Press.

Random House, Inc.:

The Random House Dictionary of the English Language, Second Edition, Unabridged. Copyright 1987 by Random House, Inc. By permission.

The Random House Guide To Good Writing. Copyright 1991 by Random House, Inc.

The Reader's Digest Association, Inc.:

Reader's Digest Success With Words. Copyright 1983 by The Reader's Digest Association.

Scott, Foresman and Company:

The Little, Brown Handbook, Fourth Edition. Copyright 1989 by Scott Foresman and Company.

The University of Chicago Press:

The Chicago Manual of Style, Thirteenth Edition. Copyright 1982 by The University of Chicago.

The Washington Post Writers Group:

William Raspberry, *The Washington Post,* February 12, 1985. By permission.

I also wish to express a special note of thanks to family friend Edith Wiles, retired teacher of senior and advanced placement English at Central High School in Knoxville, Tennessee. She reviews all of my copy for any "gremlins" it might contain prior to publication and provides invaluable assistance.

And I would be remiss if I failed to mention the late Miss Ada Branson, whose excellent instruction in the eighth and ninth grades gave me a solid foundation in the English language.

I also am grateful to all those who, through the years, have passed along suggestions for articles and to those who posed questions that resulted in articles.

Foremost among those providing suggestions were my wife, our two daughters, and our two sons-in-law, all of whom have a keen awareness of grammar, usage, and punctuation.

CONTENTS

INTRODUCTION

This book is the result of a lot of note-taking—short notes I made to myself over a period of several years when I would read or hear a mistake in grammar or word usage and when I would see an incorrect use of a punctuation mark. It seemed to me that the same mistakes were being made by many people over and over again.

Eventually, I had so many notes that I thought I ought to do something with them, such as shape them into a form that would be helpful to perhaps my daughters and my grandchildren in years to come. Finally, my "Grammar Gremlins" newspaper column evolved and now this book.

The material presented here deals with everyday problems in grammar, usage, and punctuation. The information is specifically not intended to read like a school lesson. I wanted it to be easy to read and to be presented in short segments.

But the information has found its way to the classroom through the teachers' groups I have spoken to. It is always gratifying to me to see the teachers taking notes about the errors that I list as occurring frequently. They explain that they want to be sure to place emphasis on these points in their classroom instruction.

The subject material comes from snippets of conversations overheard on the street, from correspondence that crossed my desk, from public speakers, from brochures and pamphlets, from newspapers, from television and radio programs, from church bulletins, advertising mailers, and even from fund-raising literature published by a school system. It seems no one is exempt.

I am often reminded there are no laws of grammar that you must obey, only rules. Your use of the English language is one of the key standards by which you are measured—socially, professionally, and academically. Yet, many Americans seem to be losing the ability to use proper grammar.

Grammar Gremlins can help you. Read some of it each day. Better still, keep it handy for quick reference. It will help you resolve those nagging little grammar questions you encounter.

SECTION 1

This section deals with punctuation, capitalization, abbreviations, and spellings.

Why is there such confusion over the use of the apostrophe? Why is the proper use of periods and commas with quotation marks such a major problem for many people?

Why is there so much confusion over the abbreviations of states? Where did this confusion begin? What is the correct name of that seasonal time change when we "spring forward" and "fall back"?

Americans have difficulty sorting out British and Latin spellings as they go about their daily work. How does Americanization of words evolve?

Answers to the questions listed here and some helpful hints on other related points are provided on the following pages.

_It's_ been a frightening day.

The truck lost _its_ tire coming down the hill.

It's—Its

The apostrophe is a devilish little punctuation mark that confuses a lot of people. It is not uncommon to see *it's* when the writer meant *its*. This is one of the most common mistakes seen in business correspondence today.

With the apostrophe, the term means *it is* or *it has*. Without the apostrophe, *its* is the possessive form of *it*, as in "The cat ate its food." Remember, if you want to say *it is* or *it has*, use the apostrophe. Otherwise, leave it out.

The *Johnsons* live here.

Nameplate Apostrophes

As you drive through the neighborhood, you see mailboxes that tell you the Johnsons or the Andersons live there. Have you noticed the spellings? Most often the name is displayed with an apostrophe in it, but this is wrong. The *apostrophe s* shows possession, as in Bill's or Mary's mailbox.

The nameplate should read: "The Johnsons" or "The Andersons"—no apostrophe. The signs are intending to say two or more Johnsons or Andersons live there—plural—not possessive. Therefore, the apostrophe is not needed.

The teacher said,

"Periods and commas are placed inside quotation marks."

Periods and Commas with Quotation Marks

Many people have trouble trying to decide whether the period and comma go inside or outside quotation marks. And when they do make the placement, they are never really certain. In American usage, the rule is simple: Periods and commas are always placed inside the quotation marks.

This rule stands even when it seems more logical to place them outside, as in writing the title of a song or television show. It appears in this instance as if the quotation marks belong to the title and should, therefore, stay with the title. But the rule holds: Periods and commas are placed inside quotation marks—always.

We thought the movie, which had been widely promoted,

would attract more people.

Commas are Handy

The comma is a convenient punctuation mark. There are rules that govern its use, but sometimes you can use it when there is no hard-and-fast rule. It's a punctuation mark that you can use just to make something clearer, but don't overdo it.

One frequent mistake in the use of the comma is to put in the first one when you want to set off a clause, then forget to put in the second one that completes the setting off.

Another place a comma is called for that people often overlook is after the year when using it in a sentence. For instance, "They will be married on July 4, 2000, a Tuesday."

The game was a difficult one for the home team,

but there are other more difficult ones yet to be played.

Commas with Conjunctions

Speech patterns sometimes affect the way some people insert commas in their writing.

More and more we are seeing commas being placed after the conjunctions *and* and *but*. Example: "We wanted to go to dinner after the program ended but, the speaker kept us far past the dinner hour."

Actually, the comma should be placed before the conjunction *but* in this example (and in any other instance when *but* and *and* link two independent clauses).

When speaking this type of sentence, many people will pause after the word *but*, and this apparently influences them when they write such sentences. They place the comma where they pause.

Many Americans travel in the <u>summer</u>, especially to the <u>state of Florida</u>.

Capitalization

Many people overuse capitalization when writing, not really knowing which words and terms should or should not be capitalized.

Perhaps these people think capitalization lends importance to what they are writing, but the use of too many capitals indicates that the writer does not really understand the rules of capitalization.

Those rules are too numerous to list here, but a few that address some of the often-seen and incorrectly used capitals are: Do not capitalize seasons of the year; do not capitalize *state* as in state of California; and do not capitalize titles such as *secretary, chairman,* and *director* when they immediately follow a personal name. For instance, it should be John Doe, "chairman of the board of directors" (all lower case).

She lives in Gary, Ind.

State Abbreviations

The two-letter abbreviations for states are a creation of the U.S. Postal Service and were intended for use only on mail, yet they show up everywhere, even on billboards.

They were designed by the postal service in the 1960s to help limit to 27 the number of characters on the city and state line of an address to facilitate the agency's electronic scanning devices. It was purely a postal invention as part of the ZIP code program, nothing more. (ZIP stands for Zone Improvement Plan.)

The old standard abbreviations, such as *Ind.* for Indiana, *Ala.* for Alabama, and *Tenn.* for Tennessee, are still correct and should be used in most instances. The postal designations for states are sometimes useful in various ways other than on mail; but when they *are* used, they should be two capital letters without periods. For instance, you should never write *In., Al.,* or *Tn.*

The conference begins at <u>8 a.m. Wednesday</u>.

The Use of A.M. and P.M.

There is a tendency by some to use *a.m.* and *morning* in the same sentence to designate the time. The use of both is superfluous. (The same applies to *p.m.* and *evening.*)

Perhaps it is a result of carelessness or a desire on the part of the user to be explicit. Whatever the reason, the use of such a phrase as "8 a.m. Thursday morning" is inappropriate.

In the use of *a.m.* and *p.m.,* the question often arises as to whether they should be lower case or capitals. Either way is acceptable, but the letters should always have periods after them and no space in between.

The title of his book is <u>Exploring the Deep</u>.

Italics

Until the advent of word processors a few years ago, those in the printing business were mostly the ones who dealt with italics.

The situation changed dramatically, though, as many software programs gave users a wide selection of type styles from which to choose.

This increased flexibility has made it appealing for typists and writers to use italics in their text for emphasis, but the use of italics should not be overdone just because the capability exists.

The rules vary, but basically, one should italicize (or underline) titles of books; movies; plays; periodicals; foreign words that are not yet part of the English language; and the names of ships, planes, and trains.

He graduated from college in <u>aught 9</u>, the class of 1909.

Year of Graduation

Those graduating will routinely say in the future that they were members of the class of '95 or '96. What will those say who graduate 10 years from now, in 2005 or 2006, and in other years of the first decade of the 21st century?

In the early 1900s, those graduating in the class of '04, for example, often referred to it as the class of "aught 4."

Aught has become a less-used word in the past century but could regain popularity in another decade when a similar pattern develops.

She said it was <u>all right</u> with her

for us to exchange work schedules.

All Right

How many times have you paused when writing the term *all right* and wondered whether it should be one word or two? Standard usage calls for two words—*all right*—but a lot of people want to use it as one word and spell it with only one *l*.

While the two-word version is more generally accepted as being correct, there is a good chance that the one-word version may eventually gain acceptance, especially since two other similar words, *already* and *altogether,* are correct spelled as one word and with one *l*.

Since they <u>traveled</u> only a short distance today,

they <u>canceled</u> their plans for tomorrow.

British Spellings

We often see words spelled with two *l*'s that are more appropriately spelled with one *l*.

Examples are: *travelled/travelling, cancelled/cancelling, modeled/modeling,* and *counselor/counselling.*

Although only one *l* is necessary, some individuals are tempted to use two *l*'s when they notice that others have done so.

The double *l* spellings are mainly British style or at best the secondary spelling preference in the United States.

Judgment spelled with an *e* inserted in the middle—*judgement*—falls into this category also. And *theater* and *center* should not be spelled *theatre* and *centre* unless you have a special reason for doing so. These spellings are mainly British.

He saw <u>in memoriam</u> on the stone.

In Absentia—In Memoriam

Absentia and *memoriam* are not easily found in a dictionary. You won't find them in the *a* and the *m* listings.

Both have *in* in front of them; so you have to look under *in* to find *in absentia* and *in memoriam*.

In absentia means "in absence; while or although not present."

In memoriam means "in memory of." Something given *in memoriam* is a memorial, not a memoriam.

The pronunciation of *absentia* occasionally trips up a speaker. It is pronounced *ab-SEN-sha* or *ab-SEN-she-uh*. Some dictionaries even say an acceptable pronunciation is *ab-sen-TEE-uh*.

The media <u>are</u> devoting a lot of time and space

to the search.

Foreign Words

The words *media, data,* and *criteria* are subjects of frequent discussions, particularly as to their correct singular and plural forms.

With foreign words such as these, what was incorrect yesterday might be correct today or soon will be correct. The rules are ever changing as usage of these and similar words becomes more popular.

Media can take a singular verb when used collectively to denote an industry. Be prepared for criticism, though, if you use it this way. *Medium,* the singular of *media,* early developed the meaning "an intervening agency" and was first applied to newspapers two centuries ago, according to *Random House Dictionary.*

Data is accepted as singular, but, depending on the specific meaning intended, is also plural. The original singular is *datum,* seldom used today.

Criteria is often used as a singular form, but it has not yet achieved acceptability as a singular. *Criterion* is the singular.

She had a <u>nerve-racking</u> experience.

Rack—Wrack

Nerve-racking is a term easily used in speech, but if you want to write it, the spelling might cause you to balk. Is it *racking* or *wracking*?

Either way is acceptable. The phrase means "extremely irritating, annoying, or trying."

Rack in this sense means "torment; anguish; violent strain."

Wrack means "to wreck." Therefore, one might declare after experiencing a nerve-wracking day that he or she is a wreck.

Ketchup is the most common spelling

and pronunciation of this word.

Ketchup

Choosing the preferred spelling and pronunciation of *ketchup* is as difficult as getting that red sauce out of the bottle.

Random House Dictionary lists three optional spellings: ketchup, catchup and catsup. Most other dictionaries also list these three options, not necessarily in the same order and sometimes interchanging the a and e as the second letter of the word.

The various pronunciations offered by most dictionaries are *ketchup, catchup,* and *katsup.*

The name derives from a Chinese word for fish brine, probably by way of the Malaysian *ketjap,* according to *Encyclopaedia Britannica.*

This word would not be such a problem if we didn't waiver just a little bit when we see or hear it used differently from the way we use it and wonder whether our choice is the correct one.

It's _saving_, not _savings_, in daylight-saving time.

Daylight-Saving Time

Changing to and from daylight-saving time is a familiar practice for all of us, yet there is often confusion about the proper name of this seasonal time change. Many mistakenly refer to it as day-light-*savings* time.

In most aspects of our lives, the use of *savings* is more typical than *saving* (a savings bond, a savings account, a savings and loan association, a savings on a bargain purchase). This familiarity with *savings* apparently is the reason many people incorrectly use it when they intend to refer to *daylight-saving time.*

An up-to-date dictionary will help with

the spelling of hyphenated words.

The Hyphen

The hyphen is the only mark of punctuation that joins words or parts of words together. In reality, it is more a mark of spelling than of punctuation.

The Chicago Manual of Style says that of 10 spelling questions "arising in writing or editing, nine are probably concerned with compound words." It is in the forming of compound words that the hyphen comes into play. Two examples of such words are *middle-aged* and *one-sided.*

Most reference books say there are several generalizations that can be made about using the hyphen in forming compound words, but these same books also say you should consult a dictionary when in doubt.

The hyphen's other use is in word division at the end of a line. The dictionary also is an excellent source for finding how to divide words at the end of a line. The basic rule is to divide only between syllables.

SECTION 2

Some of the basics of grammar are discussed in this section, points such as agreement, misplaced modifiers, run-on or fused sentences, and placement of prepositions.

Do you insert the word *only* in the wrong place in a sentence? Is it wrong to end a sentence with a preposition? Does your writing contain run-on or fused sentences? Do you change from first person to third person in the same sentence?

This section discusses these points and related ones.

_We_ are pleased to announce

our relocation to _our_ new office.

Person

The rules of grammar governing the use of first, second, and third person in speech and writing apparently are difficult for some people to remember.

Many will shift from first person to third person in the same sentence.

A postcard announcement mailed by a company read: XYZ "Company [third person] is pleased to announce its [third person] relocation to our [first person] newly acquired corporate offices." *Our* should be changed to *its*.

First person represents the speaker, second person represents the person(s) spoken to, and third person represents the person(s) or thing(s) spoken about.

She is one of those women who are [not is]

forming a new company.

The Use of One

The word *one* is so obviously singular that the use of it would seem always to call for a singular verb.

But such is not the case when a sentence contains the clause "one of those who (or that or which). . . ."

A sentence containing this clause calls for a plural rather than a singular verb. For instance, "She is one of those women who are forming a new company."

Who refers to the plural *women*. Therefore, the verb should be the plural *are* rather than the singular *is*. But the feeling that *one* is the subject is so strong that there is a tendency by many to use *is* rather than *are*.

If you insert the words *the only* in front of *one* in such constructions, the verb should be singular because the *who* refers to one. Example: "She is *the only* one of those women who *is* forming a new company."

The firm is observing <u>its</u> 50th anniversary.

They—It

Many people use *they* instead of *it* when referring to a company. But is this correct?

If the company name (a noun) is singular, a singular pronoun ordinarily would be required when referring to the company—*it* instead of *they.* Example: "Zebra Plumbing is growing. It made a big profit last year."

Here is an example using the plural sense: "I asked Zebra Plumbing about the job, and they will give me an estimate."

Webster's Dictionary of English Usage says: "Names of companies and other organizations function like other collective nouns, being sometimes singular and sometimes plural."

If we think of the company as a group of individuals combining their efforts to do a job, the plural *they* is acceptable even though the company name is singular.

Let's you and <u>me</u> go to the game.

Let's You and Me . . .

"Let's you and me go to the game." Or is it "you and I"?

The *me* version conforms to the traditional rules of grammar. *Let's* is a contraction for *let us.* Since *us* is the objective form, the explanatory pronouns identifying *us*—you and me—are also objective, according to *The Gregg Reference Manual.*

For instance, leave out *us* and say it. It would be *let me,* not *let I.* Therefore, it is *let's you and me.* Regardless of the traditional rules, *Random House Dictionary* says the *I* version is more popular.

Constructions such as "Let's us wash the car" clearly are redundant. What is being said is "Let us us wash the car." The *let's us* expressions, however, are usually limited to casual conversation and are not common in formal writing or speech.

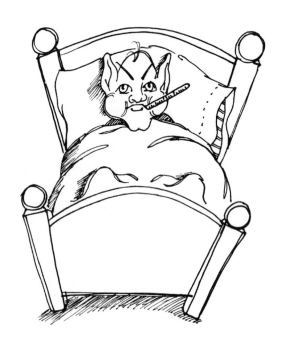

Dr. Smith has a poor bedside manner,

<u>but</u> that doesn't bother me.

Odd Formations

Odd sentence formations sometimes occur in a person's speech, whereas the same constructions would not appear in his or her writing.

These constructions often result when the speaker adds to his or her thought in midsentence.

A top-rated vocalist being interviewed on the radio said, "I was accused of being rowdy, which I was rowdy." He could have omitted the second *rowdy* if he had realized quickly enough that it was unnecessary.

Another example: "Dr. Smith has a poor bedside manner, which that doesn't bother me." (*Which* should be changed to *but,* or the word *that* should be eliminated.)

Alert speakers recognize this problem early enough in the sentence to avoid the poor construction. Unfortunately, many do not, and sentences such as the above examples result.

They gave a wonderful reception for Hillary and <u>me</u>.

I—Me

A point on which President Clinton is often criticized has nothing to do with his governmental policies. It is his use of *I* instead of *me* as part of a compound object.

Example: "They gave a wonderful reception for Hillary and I." (It should be "for Hillary and me.") Without the name, it would be "for her and me."

Someone has said that it is characteristic of residents of the Arkansas community in which Clinton spent his youth to use *I* instead of *me* as the object of a preposition.

But this misuse reaches farther than the borders of Arkansas. It is seen and heard daily in all parts of the country. Such errors result from hypercorrection—the substitution of a wrong form that is thought by the writer or speaker to be the correct form because of a misunderstanding or misapplication of a grammatical rule.

The Clinton error would be easy to avoid by just imagining the pronoun standing alone: "They gave a wonderful reception for I."

Few would use such a sentence. By doing this little test, it becomes obvious that the correct compound object should be "for Hillary and me."

I saw her <u>only</u> one time last year.

Misplaced Modifiers

Some people have a tendency to misplace certain modifiers in sentences.

Such sentences look and sound all right to users who are accustomed to the practice and do not recognize the problem. But it is obvious to many others.

Examples: "I only saw him one time last year," and "She only had five minutes remaining."

In these examples, *only* should be placed before the words *one* and *five*.

Misplaced modifiers can sometimes change the entire meaning of a sentence. For instance, there is a lot of difference between *half a fried chicken* and *a half-fried chicken.*

What was that all <u>about</u>?

Preposition at End

The best-learned grammar *rule* of all time probably is the one that says a sentence should not be ended with a preposition. Unfortunately, it is not a rule.

Examples of sentences ending with prepositions: "That's the club he belongs to." "She knows the area I am from."

Random House Dictionary says: "The often heard but misleading rule that a sentence should not end with a preposition is transferred from Latin, where it is an accurate description. But English grammar is different from Latin grammar, and the rule does not fit English."

Hodges' Harbrace College Handbook says: "The preposition may follow rather than precede its object, and it may be placed at the end of the sentence."

If you've already requested one, there's no need

to reorder. It's probably on its way to you now.

Run-on Sentences

Fused or run-on sentences often creep into hastily prepared letters, making the writers appear amateurish.

The following sentence was used in a letter mailed by one of the nation's largest companies: "If you've already requested one, there's no need to reorder, it's probably on its way to you now." In this sentence, the comma after *reorder* is insufficient. One solution would be to use a period or semicolon in place of the comma. A period would require, of course, that the beginning of the next sentence be capitalized.

Another solution would be to insert the conjunction *because* after *reorder,* leaving the comma.

There are several ways to avoid fused sentences. The careful writer will find one.

The man <u>who</u> wanted to talk with you is here.

That—Who

Is it permissible to use *that* instead of *who* or *whom* when referring to persons?

The Associated Press Stylebook says no, but other books say it is all right to do so.

The American Heritage Dictionary of the English Language, Third Edition, says: "It is entirely acceptable to write either *the man that wanted to talk to you* or *the man who wanted to talk to you.*"

The Associated Press Stylebook says to use *who* or *whom* when referring to a human being or animal with a name and to use *that* when referring to an inanimate object or animal without a name.

Random House Dictionary of the English Language says the choice of whether to use *that* or *who* or *whom* in these instances can be freely made on the basis of the sound of the sentence and one's own personal preference.

Despite the approval given by some authorities, be prepared for criticism if you use *that* instead of *who* or *whom* when referring to persons.

It was the book on manners <u>that</u> provided the correct information.

Which—That

A professor said recently that one of the biggest problems his students have in writing is knowing when to use *which* and *that*.

A clause starting with *that* generally introduces essential information. It identifies. Example: We gave the food to the dog that lives next door. (Which dog? The one that lives next door.)

Which can be used for both essential and nonessential clauses. Example with an essential clause: The dog ate the food which was placed before him. An example with a nonessential clause: The food, which consisted of table scraps, was given to the dog.

Surveys have shown that in three-fourths of the instances in which *which* is used in a clause, the clause is an essential one.

Who was it [that] told us about the play?

That Omitted

The word *that* is very versatile. With all its possible uses, it therefore seems strange that the word would be omitted anywhere it could be used. But this omission occurs.

For instance, "Who was it told us about the show?" Or "A man works here repairs antique furniture."

That should be inserted before *told* and before *works* in these two examples.

Random House Dictionary says this omission is usually considered nonstandard, but it adds that such constructions are heard even from educated speakers.

Between you and <u>me</u>, I think they are already married.

Between You and Me

The commonplace phrase *between you and me* doesn't sound right to many people, so they choose to end it with *I*.

The *me* ending is correct. Most grammar and stylebooks are firm on this point, but *Webster's Dictionary of English Usage* is a bit lenient on it.

Webster's Usage says: "You are probably safe in retaining *between you and I* in your casual speech if it exists there naturally." But *Webster's Usage* warns that the *I* version should be avoided in writing.

The rule governing this usage is that pronouns that follow prepositions must be in the objective case. *Me* is objective, and *I* is subjective. That is, *me* serves as an object, *I* as a subject. Therefore, it's *between you and me* since the preposition *between* must be followed by an object, *me*.

Foods <u>like</u> fruits and vegetables are good for us.

Like for—Such as

Some authorities on usage run up a red flag on the use of *like* and *such* as interchangeably. But others say it really doesn't make any difference which one is used.

Example: Foods such as (or like) fruits and vegetables are good for our health.

Those who insist the two should not be used the same way say *such as* should be used to indicate that the example is representative of the thing being mentioned and *like* to illustrate resemblance to the thing being mentioned.

Sample uses: "John's garden is full of nourishing vegetables, such as beans, carrots, and peas [examples of vegetables]." And "John's garden is full of those vegetables that make good, old-fashioned meals like those my grandmother used to cook [resemblance]."

Webster's Dictionary of English Usage says usage authorities Theodore Bernstein and Wilson Follett think the example-resemblance distinction is too fine to worry about, and then adds that it agrees.

It was a̱ historic moment.

A *or An with H*

Should the article *a* or *an* be used with *historic* and *historian*?

The decision sometimes is not easy because stylebooks vary on this point. The widely regarded *Associated Press Stylebook* specifies *a* before *historic*.

The basic rule is that *an* is used before a vowel sound (an owl, an eyeful), *a* before a consonant sound (a car, a tree) *and* before an *h* that is sounded (house, heart).

The *h* in *historic* and *historian* is only weakly sounded, and this lends to the varying opinions about which article should be used with them.

Some *h* words (herb, humble) can be pronounced either way, by sounding the *h* or by not sounding it ('erb, 'umble). In these instances, you may choose the article that suits your pronunciation.

I'll be back in <u>half an hour</u>.

Half an Hour

The various options in referring to a 30-minute period can cause some people to wonder which way is correct.

Two uses are *half an hour* and *a half-hour.*

Some people tend to use *a* before *half an hour,* but it is unnecessary. Correct usage is, for instance, "I'll be back in half an hour," not "a half an hour." Equally acceptable is "I'll be back in a half-hour."

The use of *a* or *an* in these constructions becomes a little troublesome.

An is used before a vowel or vowel sound and *a* is used before a consonant.

Therefore, you would use *an* in *half an hour* because *hour* begins with a vowel sound (*o*). But you would use *a* when saying *half-hour.*

Their <u>mothers-in-law</u> accompanied them.

In-law Forms

Properly distinguishing between the plural and the singular possessive form of compound nouns is sometimes confusing.

The *in-law* forms are probably the ones that most people deal with more frequently.

For most compound nouns, the plural is formed by adding an *s* to the principal word—*mothers*-in-law, *fathers*-in-law. An example: "The fathers-in-law of the three were friends."

The singular possessive form of each of these is *mother-in-law's* and *father-in-law's*. An example: "My mother-in-law's kitchen is large."

In some government offices there is the term *deputy-in-charge,* which in the plural becomes *deputies-in-charge.* An example of the singular possessive is: "The deputy-in-charge's trip was postponed."

Most all the members voted for Susan.

Most—Almost

Most as a shortened form of *almost* has been around a long time.

It is "actually good American English but is simply not accepted as such by a large body of opinion," according to *Reader's Digest Success With Words.*

Most is used to modify the adjectives *all, every,* and *any,* pronouns such as *anybody, everyone,* and others, and the adverbs *always, everywhere,* and *anywhere.*

"If you want to be on the safe side, don't use it [*most*] in formal writing," *Success With Words* says. But it adds, "If, on the other hand, you feel strong-minded about it," it is a "perfectly justifiable" use.

He arrived far too late, <u>plus</u> he forgot his report.

The Use of Plus

Much has been written about the word *plus* and whether it is acceptable in certain senses.

It is a handy and popular word in speech, but its use in some written forms can draw criticism.

Sometimes it is used as a conjunction to link two clauses. Example: "He arrived far too late, plus he forgot his report." Here it is a substitute for *and.*

Other times, *plus* is used as an adverb to introduce a sentence. Example: "Plus, every member is planning to attend, so the meeting should be successful."

These uses in formal writing have been criticized, but this criticism doesn't seem to affect their popularity in speech.

You [have] got to buy more gas.

Have Got

How many times have you heard or used such sentences as "You got to buy more gas," meaning "You must do so"? The word *have* is omitted before *got.*

Such usage is common in speech but not in writing. *Random House Dictionary* says such sentences are "characteristic of the most relaxed, informal speech."

Gotta is a pronunciation spelling of this use.

This point leads directly to the question of using *have got.* Such use is criticized by some as redundant on the grounds that *have* alone expresses the meaning adequately. For instance, "I have got five cards in my collection"; "I have five cards in my collection."

Random House Dictionary says *have got* is "well established and fully standard in all varieties of speech and writing."

More <u>importantly</u>, your comments

convinced him he should attend.

More Importantly

When you hear someone use *more importantly* and your preference is *more important,* do you wonder which is correct?

Actually, neither use is incorrect. It is a matter of preference.

Much has been written about this usage, but *American Heritage Dictionary, Third Edition,* says: "There is no obvious reason for preferring one or the other."

What about *firstly*? Example: "Firstly, I want to thank John for all he has done."

This usage has also been the subject of much controversy among English experts, but *Webster's Dictionary of English Usage* says these experts today "admit that *firstly* is all right, but they still prefer that you not use it. They want you to use *first* because it is shorter."

First is more popular than *firstly,* but regardless of your choice, you should be consistent. Example: *First, second, third,* etc., or *firstly, secondly, thirdly,* etc.

<u>Hopefully</u>, they will get a new map before their trip.

Hopefully

Those who write about grammar and usage have to address at some point the use of *hopefully* and *irregardless.* The use of these two words just does annoy many people.

The two words are discussed in practically every usage book that you pick up.

There is mixed comment on *hopefully.* Some books say avoid it. Others say it has gained acceptability and is fully standard in all varieties of speech and writing as a sentence modifier meaning "it is hoped that. . . ." Generally, you will be safe in using it, but be aware that it is criticized by many.

Irregardless does not fare so well. Most books on usage say to avoid it and use *regardless* in its place. *Irregardless* has two negative elements, *ir* and *less,* making it nonstandard.

He was waiting <u>for</u> the others to arrive.

Waiting On or For

If you delay a meeting to await someone's arrival, are you *waiting for* or *waiting on* that person?

Although the *on* version is often considered objectionable in standard usage, it is used in a large part of the country, especially in speech.

Standard usage calls for *waiting for* in the sense of waiting for someone or something to arrive.

Waiting on should be used in the sense of serving someone, as in a restaurant. Incidentally, the occupations of those who wait on you are *waitering* and *waitressing*. Example: "She did waitressing to supplement her income."

I don't know <u>whether</u> [or not] I will attend.

Whether—If

The conjunctions *whether* and *if* look very different, but they have similar uses.

For example, "I don't know whether I will go," and "I don't know if I will go."

Random House Dictionary says the use of *if* for *whether* is sometimes criticized but adds "the usage has been established in standard English for a long time."

The question often arises as to whether the words *or not* should be included after *whether,* as in this very sentence. The use of *or not* is optional.

Neither the players <u>nor</u> the coaches

expected such a close game.

Or—Nor

Should *neither* be followed by *or* or *nor* when it is used as a conjunction?

The answer is that it is almost always followed by *nor* when used as a conjunction. Examples: "Neither the players nor (not *or*) the coaches expected such a close game." "Neither the man nor his dog saw the car coming."

In addition to being a conjunction, *neither* is also an adjective and a pronoun. An example of it as an adjective is: "Neither man was running." An example of it as a pronoun is: "Bill and Sue are team workers. Neither is looking for individual recognition."

Please contact John and <u>me</u> about the work.

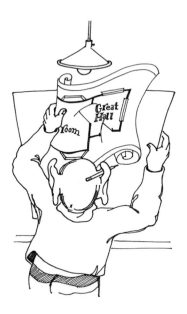

Myself—Me

Do you say *myself* when you should use *me*? Many do, but it's not the best choice. Some even say it's wrong.

You should not say, "Please contact John and myself about the work." Leave out John and see how it sounds: "Please contact myself about the work." You probably wouldn't use such a sentence.

Therefore, what you should say is, "Please contact John and me."

The pronoun *me* is perfectly good, but more and more people seem to be hesitant to use it. *Myself* generally should not be used as a substitute for *I* or *me*. It's fine, however, if you want to use it to provide emphasis to *I* or *me*. For instance, "I will do this job myself."

SECTION 3

General usage problems are addressed in this section—words, clauses, and terminology that are part of everyday speech.

We tend to use language and punctuation that we hear and see others use, but sometimes those others are wrong.

Do you have lazy speech habits? For instance, when you say *get*, does it sound more like *git*?

Do you use *promise* when you mean *honest*?

These habits and similar ones are discussed on the following pages.

<u>There're</u> five cars in the show.

There Are

A common error in grammar today is the use of *there's* when it should be *there are*.

There's is a combination of *there* and *is*. You should say, for instance, "There *are* five cars in the show," not "there *is* five cars in the show." And this latter clause is what you are really saying when you use *there's*. *Cars* is plural and requires the plural *are*.

It's lazy speech to say *there's* when you should be using *there are*.

She became <u>flustered</u> when her papers fell to the floor.

Flustered

Those who use *flusterated* or *flustrated* when they probably mean *flustered* likely will be thought to have committed an error.

Although *flusterated* and *flustrated* are listed in some of the newer dictionaries, one probably should avoid using them except in a very informal situation. They are generally viewed as make-do words.

These various versions all mean "agitated confusion."

Now, a very similar-sounding word—*frustrated*—is different. It means "to prevent from accomplishing a goal."

It <u>doesn't</u> matter.

The Use of Don't

How many times have you heard the following? "He don't want one." Or, "It don't matter." This is sloppy usage that too many people are guilty of.

We even hear it in song lyrics, but this doesn't give it acceptability. *Don't* is a combination of *do* and *not*. Most people would find it difficult to say "He do not want one" or "It do not matter." But that's really what they are saying when they say "He don't. . ." and "It don't. . ."

The proper usage is *doesn't*. It is just as easy, and it sounds a whole lot better.

All <u>told</u> [not <u>tolled</u>], there were 10 vehicles

in the pileup.

All Told

"Which is correct, 'all told' or 'all tolled' "? a reader asked.

"All told, there were 10 vehicles in the pile-up" is the correct way to say it, not *tolled.*

Told in this use is the past tense of *tell,* which means "to count." Think of "bank teller."

Webster's Ninth New Collegiate Dictionary has the entry "all told" and defines it with this phrase: "with everything taken into account: in all."

The Oxford English Dictionary also has an "all told" entry and defines it with this clause: "when all are counted." An illustrative sentence given at the entry is: "The hands numbered 19 all told."

The man drove <u>past</u> slowly.

Passed—Past

It seems that there should be little confusion between *passed* and *past,* but choosing the correct one sometimes causes even alert writers to pause. The two words sound the same.

Passed is the past tense of *pass.* Example: "I asked her to pass the salt, but she passed the pepper instead."

Past as a noun refers to time gone by, and as an adjective it means something "having already happened." A noun example: "He dwells on the past." An adjective example: "She got a raise this past year."

Past also is an adverb. Example: "The man drove past slowly." And *past* is a preposition. Example: "She went past the house."

Plans are <u>under way</u> for the new building.

Under Way

"When I change *underway* to two words—*under way*—in letters I proof for others, they think I am being nitpicking," a reader said.

"Which way *is* correct?" she asked, seeking reassurance.

Webster's Dictionary of English Usage says there is an increasing tendency in recent years to write *under way* as one word and that it might eventually predominate over the two-word form, "but for the time being *under way* is still somewhat more common."

The Associated Press Stylebook says *under way* should be "two words in virtually all uses" and "one word only when used as an adjective before a noun in a nautical sense: *an underway flotilla.*"

The everyday use, though, intends to convey the idea that something is in progress. Example: "Plans are under way for the new building."

A <u>lot</u> of people came to the party.

A Lot—Lots

A *lot of* and *lots* are popular terms in speech, but they still draw criticism from some when used in formal writing.

Critics say *many, a great many,* or *much* should be used instead in formal contexts.

A *lot of* and *lots of* are so convenient to use that one can easily develop a pattern of overusing them.

Then, what naturally follows is that some, when writing *a lot,* run the two words together into *alot,* which is a common enough error that it is addressed in a few grammar and usage books.

Webster's Dictionary of English Usage says this misspelling occurs "perhaps by people in a hurry."

The original model was poorly made

and the new one is <u>equally</u> bad.

Equally As

The use of the phrase *equally as* was criticized by a reader, and the criticism was appropriate. *The Associated Press Stylebook* is very clear on this point. It says: "Do not use the words together; one is sufficient."

Webster's Dictionary of English Usage describes the phrase as "idiomatic" and says it occurs commonly in speech but adds, "its reputation is bad enough to make it relatively rare in edited prose."

Webster's Usage also says: "This innocuous phrase has drawn more vehement criticism than is warranted, but you may well want to prefer *just as* in your writing or to use *equally* by itself. . . ."

A __man__ was arrested in the murder case.

Gentleman—Lady

A New York police official announced on national television that a "gentleman" had been arrested in a major killing.

A few days later, a news report from another part of the country said a "lady" had been arrested and jailed in an incident.

In this day of gender awareness, it was surprising to hear and see these two terms used in instances in which they could have and should have been avoided.

The Associated Press Stylebook says of these two words: "Do not use [*gentleman*] as a synonym for *man,* and do not use [*lady*] as a synonym for *woman.*"

Rosalie Maggio in her book *The Bias-Free Word Finder* condemns both *gentleman* and *lady* except in the context of the "still-acceptable generic public address of 'ladies and gentlemen' and for an occasional, 'He is a real gentleman.' "

The American Heritage Dictionary, Third Edition, published in 1992, says *gentleman* and *lady* are "properly used . . . in order to emphasize norms expected in civil society or in situations requiring civil courtesies."

She gave testimony about the event.

Sworn Testimony

With court stories so common in the news and in movies, we are frequently exposed to the terms *testimony* and *deposition.*

Often the word *sworn* is used in front of these words, but it is unnecessary.

In the field of law, *testimony* is defined as statements of a witness "under oath" in a court or before an official body.

A *deposition* is testimony or a statement under oath that is taken down in writing for use later in a court or before an official body.

To qualify as testimony or a deposition in the field of law, these statements must be under oath—a solemn pledge in which one swears to speak the truth. Therefore, the use of *sworn* in front of these words is redundant.

I am going to get [me] some cash.

Get Me

A reader asked about the use of *me* instead of *myself* in the following sense: "I am going to get me some cash."

The use of *me* in this sense—as an indirect object—is common, but it is used more in speech than in formal writing.

The same thing can be said of *you,* as in "Did you get you a new supply of firewood?" In formal writing, *yourself* should be used in place of the second *you.*

In both examples, the use of these indirect objects is actually unnecessary. For instance, "I am going to get some cash." And "Did you get a new supply of firewood?"

Can [may] I get anything else for you?

Can—May

A reader said he heard *can* used recently and thought the use should have been *may*.

The use was, "Can I get anything else for you?"

Are these two words—*can* and *may*—interchangeable? In the strictest sense, no, but the rule is seldom applied.

Can expresses possibility, and *may* expresses permission.

Webster's Ninth New Collegiate Dictionary says: "The use of *can* to ask or grant permission has been common since the 19th century and is well established."

Random House Dictionary says sentences using *can* in the permission sense occur mainly in speech and in informal writing, whereas *may* occurs in this sense more in formal contexts.

The shops were <u>really close</u> to the houses.

Real Close

A billboard message that used *real close* and *real easy* in advertising a shopping mall drew criticism from a few passersby.

They said it should have been *really close* and *really easy*, and they were correct—technically. An adjective *(real)* cannot modify an adverb *(close* and *easy)*.

Even so, books on usage say that *real* is widely used in informal speech to mean *very*. Such use is not appropriate in formal writing, but it is accepted in informal writing, such as is seen on billboards.

Webster's Dictionary of English Usage says even though the use of *real* for *very* is more likely to be encountered in speech, "it has spread considerably in general writing."

They came to the <u>exact same</u> conclusion.

Exact Same

A reader asked about the use of *exact same* and questioned its correctness.

This is one of those redundant terms that are popular with many people, especially in speech, to emphasize a point. Others are *past history, end result,* and *continue on* (which was questioned by another reader).

Webster's Dictionary of English Usage says criticism of these types of redundancies can be "taken with a large grain of salt," that is, with skepticism.

Webster's Usage says it is all right to use these types of expressions. "Feel free to judge for yourself where they may be useful" or where they "simply sound better" than the use of just one of the words.

Be aware, however, that the use of *exact same* or any of the other similar terms will draw criticism from some.

He, <u>too</u>, is planning to be on vacation next week.

The Use of Too

When *too* is used at the end of a clause or a sentence, a comma does not precede it. Example: Our sales have increased too.

If *too* meaning *also* occurs elsewhere in a sentence, particularly between the subject and verb, it is set off by commas. Example: He, too, is planning to be on vacation next week.

Of course, when *too* is used to mean *excessive,* it is not set off by commas. Example: She was too late to see the opening of the play.

Someone entered the room.

Someone—Somebody

A reader asked which is correct or preferred, *someone* or *somebody.*

It used to be that *somebody* was used more frequently than *someone,* but in the 20th century, *someone* has come on strong, according to *Webster's Dictionary of English Usage,* and it is now slightly preferred over *somebody.*

Webster's Usage says both "are equally standard" and that you may "use whichever one you think sounds better in a given context."

These two pronouns take a singular verb but are often referred to by the plural pronouns *they, their,* and *them.* Example: "Someone left. I saw them walk out."

Webster's Usage says: "When the speaker or writer has more than one person in mind, or a very indefinite somebody, the plural pronoun tends to be used." Example: "Somebody told me they thought he died."

An example with a singular pronoun: "Someone is making a speech, but he is almost finished."

I went to the <u>drive-thru</u> window.

Thru—Through

Drive-through service is well established in our society, but this spelling of the term is not the one we usually see. Most often it is spelled *drive-thru*, especially at fast-food restaurants.

Random House Dictionary lists *thru* as "an informal, simplified spelling of *through*."

Webster's Ninth New Collegiate Dictionary lists *thru* as a variant of *through*.

Webster's Dictionary of English Usage says *thru* has never been "less than standard, but it remains a distant second choice in print."

Other than on the *drive-thru* signs, *thru* shows up mainly in catalogs and programs where space is limited.

Thruway though, for *highway,* is well established.

The stores are open <u>till</u> midnight.

Till—Until

Till and *until* are good words and may be used interchangeably, but what about *'til*?

Webster's Dictionary of English Usage says *'til* is used by those who do not know that *till* is a complete, unabbreviated word in its own right.

The use of *'til* is common in casual writing, and it is often used in advertising and on signs. Example: "Shop 'til 9."

Oddly enough, *American Heritage Dictionary, Third Edition,* says *'til* is considered acceptable even though it is technically incorrect.

Nonetheless, *till* or *until* should be used in formal writing. *Till* is not a shortened version of *until*; therefore, the use of an apostrophe with *till* (*'till*) is incorrect.

The annoying sound kept <u>recurring</u>.

Recur—Reoccur

Is it correct to use *reoccur*? We often hear it instead of *recur.*

The Associated Press Stylebook rejects *reoccur* and specifies *recur, recurred,* and *recurring.*

Webster's Dictionary of English Usage says both are good words but that *recur* and *recurrence* are preferred by most writers. So what is the difference?

Webster's Usage says: "*Reoccur* and *reoccurrence* are the more basic words: they simply tell you that something happened again." Some suggest that the use of these two forms implies that there has been only one repetition, but *Webster's Usage* says the use suggests nothing about the number of repetitions.

Webster's Usage says, however, that "*recur* and especially *recurrence* can suggest a periodic or frequent repetition" as well as a onetime repetition.

I bought it <u>off</u> [<u>from</u>] a street vendor.

Off—From

A reader asks how a batter can get a "hit off a pitcher." She adds, "It seems to be an almost impossible thing to do if you look at what the phrase says."

Random House Dictionary lists several definitions and uses of the word *off*. One of these says *off* meaning "from a specific source" is informal. For example, "I bought it off a street vendor."

Webster's Dictionary of English Usage says: "There is nothing wrong with *off* in the sense of *from*, although it is perhaps more often a speech form than a written one and to many people it will suggest uneducated speech."

Webster's Usage adds: "So, while the objection may have no rational foundation, you should at least be aware that it exists."

She graduated <u>from</u> college in 1994.

Graduated From

The proper way to express the verb *graduate* has long been debated.

It is best always to use *from*.

Examples: "She graduated *from* college in 1994."

"She *was* graduated *from* college in 1994." (It is not necessary to use *was,* as in the preceding sentence, but it is not wrong if you do.)

You should never say, "She graduated college in 1994." Stylebooks say constructions with *from* in them are the most common.

I don't think he is here.

Shifting the Negative

You have used sentences similar to the following many times but probably never paused to consider the lack of logic in them:

"I do not believe I want to go."

Actually, the user is intending to say, "I believe I do not want to go."

This change in wording is called shifting the negative. The negative *do not* logically should be placed next to the verb *want*.

This shifting of the negative occurs commonly in expressions involving *think, believe, seem,* and *suppose*.

Those who object to such constructions say they are illogical, and they are. But they have been with us a long time and are here to stay.

Where is he [at]?

Where At

Use *where at* or some similar phrase and you are certain to be criticized. "It will be hard to score from where the ball's at."

Such usage is rarely seen in writing, but it does crop up in the speech of some in a large part of the country.

Webster's Dictionary of English Usage says authorities have for years condemned such usage but notes that it would be "entirely futile to attempt to eradicate a speech form by denouncing it in books on writing."

"And a more harmless idiom [an expression peculiar to itself] would be hard to imagine," *Webster's Usage* adds.

The *at* provides a word at the end of a sentence that can be given stress, and this might be the reason some people use it.

Their children were <u>reared</u> in Ohio.

Raise—Rear

Whether to use *raise* or *rear* in referring to the upbringing of children has long been debated.

My observation is that *raise* has overtaken *rear* in popularity, particularly with young adults, many of whom do not feel comfortable using *rear* in this sense. They consider it old-fashioned.

Many dictionaries say either use is correct.

Random House Dictionary of the English Language addresses this issue directly: "Both *raise* and *rear* are used in the United States to refer to the upbringing of children. Although *raise* was formerly condemned in this sense, it is now standard."

She doesn't use the manual often; however,

I think she will eventually learn the new procedures.

However—But

There is a tendency by some to use *however* incorrectly in a sentence by using it the same way they use *but.*

Sentences such as the following are seen often: "She doesn't use the revised manual often, however, I think she will eventually learn the new procedures."

If *but* were used instead of *however,* the comma after *often* is all that would be necessary. But since *however* does not function in the same way as *but,* a period or semicolon is required after *often.*

Used as it is in the example sentence, *however* serves as a conjunctive adverb. The function of such a word is to relate two main clauses, but because the two main clauses remain independent, a comma is an insufficient separation of the two.

But is different in that it is a coordinating conjunction and is used to link two words or word groups of the same kind. Only a comma is required before it.

He was <u>hanged</u> for the murders.

Hanged—Hung

The legal hanging execution in the state of Washington in 1993—at that time, the first in this country in 28 years—once again focused attention on the age-old discussion of the use of *hanged* versus *hung*.

In short, *hanged* is preferred by most usage authorities for referring to an official execution.

But if someone hangs himself or another person, either intentionally or accidentally, it is acceptable to use *hung* to describe the act.

Webster's Dictionary of English Usage says the use of *hung* is more likely than *hanged* when the hanging described is in effigy.

The following examples give pure past tense uses of *hang:* "The boy hung from the swing by his heels" and "The artist hung her painting."

Honestly, that's the way it happened.

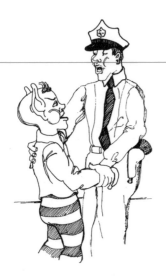

Promise—Honest

"I promise you, that's the way it happened."
Some people will sometimes use the word
promise in the above sense to refer to something in
the past. *Promise* pertains to the future, not the past.
The above declaration would be more appropriate as follows: "Honestly, that's the way it happened." This is really what the speaker is intending
to say, meaning "truthfully and sincerely."

If you are looking forward to an event, are
you *eager* or *anxious* for it to happen?

The use of these words interchangeably is
sometimes criticized, but *Random House Dictionary*
says that while some insist that *anxious* must always
convey a sense of distress or worry, its use in the
sense of *eager* is fully standard.

She was hesitant to step on the <u>scales</u>.

Scales—Scale

The words *scales* and *scissors* are tricky because they look and sound plural but are singular.

The object used for weighing is a *scale* or *scales,* both singular, but if you are referring to more than one, you would also say *scales.*

Scissors is often used with *pair of.* To denote more than one, you would say "two pairs of scissors."

If you cut something with scissors, you *scissor* it. Of course, you can *scale* something too, but that usage has an entirely different meaning from *weigh.*

He <u>mightn't</u> attend.

Mightn't

In his hit song "Achy Breaky Heart," Billy Ray Cyrus uses a word that is worth mentioning here just because of the way he says it. The word is *might,* but two of the five times he uses *might,* he adds a syllable to it that makes it sound like *mightn't.* The phrase in point follows:

"And if you tell my heart, my achy breaky heart, / he might blow up and kill this man."

The contraction *mightn't* means *might not.* Cyrus obviously does not mean it this way, but his added syllable makes it sound like *mightn't.*

Constructions similar to *mightn't* include *oughtn't,* a contraction of *ought not; mustn't,* a contraction of *must not;* and, of course, several others.

They obtained their <u>licenses</u> the same year.

License

The word *license* is singular but sounds plural because of the s sound on the end. This causes some people occasionally to refer to a license in a plural sense.

An example is: "The notice for my driver's license came. I'm going to get them renewed tomorrow." (You should say "get it renewed.") If you are referring to more than one license, you would use *licenses.*

License is also a verb. A company can license you to sell products, and in doing so, licenses you.

Do not pronounce <u>get</u> as <u>git</u>.

Get—Git

The use of *git* for *get* quickly labels someone making a formal speech. The user sounds very unprofessional.

But listen to yourself and those around you. Many educated people fail to enunciate *get* in their everyday speech, using a pronunciation that sounds more like *git*.

This informal pattern of speech can sometimes be hard to overcome when one wants to sound formal.

Such a fate befell a nationally prominent female when she spoke to a women's group. In excerpts of her speech that were telecast by the networks, most of her uses of *get* came across as something closer to *git*.

Nothing was ever said or written about her inappropriate pronunciation of *get,* but it must have been noticed by many.

They were <u>enthused</u> by his response.

Enthuse

The verb *enthused* is handy, but it can draw criticism. It is described by some dictionaries as colloquial. *The Oxford English Dictionary* is rather harsh in its definition, ". . .an ignorant back-formation from enthusiasm."

Random House Dictionary, however, says: "Enthuse is now standard and well established in the speech and all but the most formal writing of educated persons." It adds: "Despite its long history and frequent occurrence, enthuse is still strongly disapproved of by many."

When using this word, just remember that there are some who will believe it is incorrect. While it does the job, it invites possible criticism.

The new students were <u>oriented</u> by the dean.

Orient—Orientate

The word *orient* is unusual in that it is popularly used in a business and professional setting but also describes a part of the world. (The latter version is capitalized.)

The real problem comes when one tries to decide whether to use *orient* or *orientate* in describing the process of acquainting someone with his or her surroundings or circumstances. And was someone *oriented* or *orientated*?

In most dictionaries, *orient* has numerous definitions and interpretations listed beside it. The word *orientate* is listed, but the only definition given is "to orient."

Orient seems to be the preferred word for describing the process of familiarizing someone with his or her surroundings.

We receive our paychecks <u>biweekly</u> [every two weeks].

Biweekly—Bimonthly

If you receive a paycheck every two weeks, are you paid bimonthly or biweekly?

These two terms are confusing to many people. Since *bi* can be understood to mean either "twice each" or "every two," it would be best to avoid both *bimonthly* and *biweekly* if you really want to be clear.

One recommendation by *Random House Dictionary* to eliminate confusion in these instances is to use *twice a* week (month, year) for one sense and *every two* weeks (months, years) for the other.

Another option for the latter sense is *every other* week (month, year).

I __couldn't__ care less about what she thinks.

Couldn't Care Less

Why is it that people often adopt and make frequent use of phrases that do not really mean what they want to say?

Two examples: "I could care less" and "I am going to try and do it."

In the first example, the user is wanting to say he or she "could *not* care less," but that is not what is said.

In the second example, the user is intending to say that he or she is "going to try *to* do it."

The odd thing about both these phrases, though, is that regardless of how they are said, the listener gets the correct message.

It's too <u>hot a day</u> to play tennis outdoors.

An Unnecessary Word

"It's too hot of a day." "How long of a drive is it?" Did you ever wonder why some people insert the preposition *of* in these types of sentences?

Such uses are largely restricted to informal speech and are not seen often in writing.

This pattern of use probably comes from the *too* and the *how* constructions that have the word *much* in them, and, according to *Random House Dictionary,* are standard uses. For instance, "There was too much of an uproar" or "How much of a problem will it be?"

The example sentences in the first paragraph (and other similar sentences) would be more effective without *of* in them.

The employees are covered by

<u>workers'</u> compensation insurance.

Workers' Replaces Workmen's

Many countries have official bodies, called academies, that establish standards for language usage, but none exists in the United States.

Official acts, though, have been passed by most states in recent years, changing a word in a term that is familiar to business and industry, making that word neuter in gender.

Workmen's compensation insurance became *workers' compensation insurance* by those acts. However, most dictionaries still use *workmen's* to identify this type of insurance.

He <u>snuck</u> past the gatekeeper.

Snuck—Sneaked

Snuck is one of those words that you feel guilty in using (instead of *sneaked*) but which seem to express the situation so well. It has gained enough stature to be acceptable in informal usage, probably more in speaking than in writing, but use it cautiously.

Random House Dictionary says: "Snuck has occasionally been considered nonstandard, but it is so widely used by professional writers and educated speakers that it can no longer be so regarded."

Some dictionaries still consider *snuck* nonstandard, though, and the use of it could evoke criticism.

Two words that have optional past tenses that are proper in either formal or informal use are *speed* and *plead*. You can correctly use *speeded* or *sped, pleaded* or *pled*.

SECTION 4

The oddities of pronunciations, the regional factors that affect the way some words are used, and generally confusing uses of certain words are described on the following pages.

For instance, is *roofs* pronounced with a *v* sound or an *f* sound at the end?

You have heard *asterisk* pronounced as if the ending is *rik*. Why does this happen?

At Christmastime, the pronunciation of *poinsettia* frequently causes puzzlement. Not long afterward comes the second month of the year. How is it pronounced?

Comments on these points are presented on the following pages.

He <u>yoost</u> to be a skydiver.

Used To

Pronounce the phrases *used to* and *supposed to*. Do you hear the *d* sound on the end of the first word of each? Probably not.

The *d* is correct, but few enunciate it. Consequently, people often pause when writing the phrases, uncertain whether to add the *d*.

In these phrases, the pronunciations often are more like *yoost* and *suppost*. Examples: "He yoost to belong to the club." "She is suppost to leave tomorrow." With *to* following so closely, it is difficult to enunciate the *d* that comes immediately before it.

Those who want to speak properly, though, will try to soften the *t* sound and use more of a *d* sound.

The basket was full of <u>gladioli</u>.

Gladiolus—Gladioli

It's easy to understand why that popular flower the *glad* is often referred to by this shortened name rather than by its full name, *gladiolus.* It's a confusing name.

"One gladiolus may make for a sparse bouquet, but at least it spares you from having to figure out what to call more than one of them," says *Webster's Dictionary of English Usage.*

Gladioli is the most common plural form of the word, but it may sound strange to some. Other accepted plurals are *gladiolus,* the same as the singular form, and *gladioluses.*

Webster's Usage says: "Happy are those for whom the word is *gladiola* and the plural *gladiolas* (though some will say that's a case of ignorance being bliss)."

The Reader's Digest Success With Words says *gladiola* should not be used in formal writing but that in everyday speech it is acceptable.

They are from <u>Illinoie</u>.

Illinois

Many people who pronounce *Illinois* as *Illinoie* probably have no idea why they do so.

What *is* the reason for the *noie* pronunciation?

The name of the state comes from the Indian word *Illini,* which was the name of the Indian tribes who first lived in that area.

French settlers there called the tribes *Illinois,* which in French has a *noie* ending sound.

Dictionaries list the *noiz* pronunciation following the *noie* entry. *Random House Dictionary* says, however, that the pronunciation with the final *z* sound "occurs chiefly among less educated speakers" and is least common in the state itself.

The *noiz* pronunciation increases in frequency as distance from the state increases, *Random House* says.

Harass can be pronounced *hair-as* or *ha-rass*.

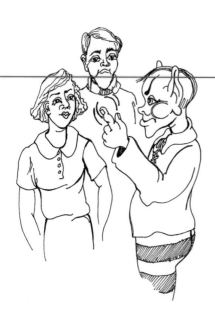

Harass

Is *harassment* pronounced *hair-asment* or *ha-rass-ment?* We hear it both ways.

Both pronunciations are acceptable, but *harass-ment* is the most frequently heard version, according to *Random House Dictionary of the English Language.*

Harass is a French word that traditionally was pronounced as if it were spelled *hair-as*. But the newer pronunciation *ha-rass* developed in this country and has become the more common one, especially with younger speakers, according to *Random House.*

The pronunciation of *controversial* presents similar problems. The last syllable can be pronounced *shul* or *see-ul*. Either way is all right. It's just a matter of preference.

Lived in short-lived can rhyme with *lift* or *dived*.

Short-lived

Is *short-lived* pronounced with a long *i* or with a short *i,* a reader of my column asked.

Then she said she uses the long *i* and added, "I think I am correct."

The long *i* pronunciation is more correct since the term is derived from the noun *life,* not from the verb *live,* as in "They will live here."

But *American Heritage Dictionary, Third Edition,* says the short *i* pronunciation is so common today that it cannot be considered an error. Dictionaries list both pronunciations.

As an indication of how acceptance of this pronunciation has changed over the years, *Webster's New International Dictionary* of 1915 listed only the long *i* pronunciation.

It is best to pronounce <u>nuclear</u> as <u>nu-kle-er</u>.

Nuclear

Every so often, the issue of the correct pronunciation of *nuclear* comes up.

A reader wrote that she almost rises from her seat in protest when she hears the word pronounced *nu-cu-ler* instead of *nu-kle-er.* Former Secretary of Defense Les Aspin and former President Jimmy Carter use the *nu-cu-ler* pronunciation, as do many others.

Success With Words by Reader's Digest says: "Those who shift a consonant in this word . . . aren't committing a grievous sin against the language; they are doing what comes naturally."

They are transposing two sounds in a word (technically known as metathesizing). For instance, the *clear* portion of *nuclear* is often pronounced *kle-yer.* If the *l* and *y* sounds are transposed, you have *nu-kya-ler.*

Further, a lot of people associate the pronunciation of *nuclear* with words such as *particular* and *muscular* and pronounce the last two syllables of *nuclear* the same as they do the last two syllables of these other words.

The horses were running <u>toward</u> us.

Toward—Towards

Is it *toward* or *towards*?

If you use one version and see or hear the other one, a question probably arises in your mind about which one is correct.

The Associated Press Stylebook says not to use *towards,* but most other books list both versions as acceptable, with *toward* being the preferred choice.

While *toward* is more common in America, the British preference is *towards.*

Some critics have tried to find a technical basis for the difference in the two forms of this word, "but there is none," according to *Webster's Dictionary of English Usage.*

He <u>burned</u> the toast.

Burned—Burnt

When verbs have two forms of past tense and past participle, they can cause confusion.

Some examples: *burned-burnt, dreamed-dreamt, leaped-leapt,* and *kneeled-knelt.*

In short, all these forms are correct, but some versions are heard and seen more frequently than others.

To use one of these verbs as an example, *burned* is more common than *burnt* whether it is used with or without an object. Example: "He burned the debris" and "the building burned."

Burnt has a slight edge in popularity as the adjective form of the word, according to *Webster's Dictionary of English Usage.* Example: "We fed the burnt toast to the birds."

You may pronounce the 0 in numbers either oh or zero.

Zero—0

One might say this is an article about nothing. Zero. 0.

When you state a telephone number containing *0*, do you say "0" as in *oh*, or do you say "zero"?

Telephone directory assistance operators have long given telephone numbers by saying *oh* for the zeros in those numbers. It is easier to write a telephone number if the person stating it for you says *oh* rather than *zero*.

One of the definitions for the letter *O* listed in *Webster's Ninth New Collegiate Dictionary* is "something shaped like the letter *O; esp: zero.*" Other dictionaries give similar definitions.

So, the decision whether to use *zero* or *oh* when stating numbers comes down to personal preference.

Pronouncing <u>ing</u> on the end of words is more formal.

-ing Endings

Those who pronounce words ending with *ing* as if they end with *in*—"runnin'," "flyin'," "workin' "—are often said to be "dropping the *g*." But no actual *g* sound is involved.

Sometimes the letter *g* is pronounced like the first letter in *gee whiz* and sometimes it is a hard *g*, such as the first *g* in *garage*. But neither of these is the same sound as is in the suffix *ing*. There is more of an *ung* sound used for the *ng* portion of the *ing*.

Random House Dictionary says many speakers use both pronunciations, *ing* and *in*, depending on the speed at which they speak and the level of formality desired, with the *ing* pronunciation being considered more formal.

Linguists say studies show the *in* ending is used more by men than by women. They say this probably has some relationship with women traditionally having concern for their images, and this attribute influences their speech habits, causing them to choose the more formal *ing*.

The spellings and pronunciations

~~*sherbert* and *sherbet* are equally correct.~~

Sherbet—Sherbert

How many times have you ordered sherbert and wondered if you should have pronounced it *sherbet*, without the second *r,* or vice versa?

Both spellings and pronunciations are recognized by *Webster's Ninth New Collegiate Dictionary* and *American Heritage Dictionary, Third Edition. Sherbert* is not recognized by *Random House Dictionary.*

Webster's Dictionary of English Usage says *sherbet* is the usual spelling. It adds that the *sherbert* pronunciation—with the sounding of the second *r*—is sometimes cited as an error, "though it can be heard from educated speakers."

Webster's Usage also says it is more common to hear the pronunciation with the second *r* than it is to see the word written with it.

Greasy can be pronounced *gre-see* or *gre-zee*.

Greasy

If you say "greasy" with a *z* sound and hear someone else pronounce it as if it were spelled *gree-see,* do you wonder if you are the one who's wrong?

Greasy is almost always pronounced with the *z* sound in the South, but you hear it more often with the *see* sound in New England, New York, and the Great Lakes area.

It is one of those words whose pronunciation depends on where you live, sort of like *pecan,* which has three pronunciations—*pe-kahn, pee-CAN,* and *PEE-can.*

Prostrate and _prostate_ have different meanings.

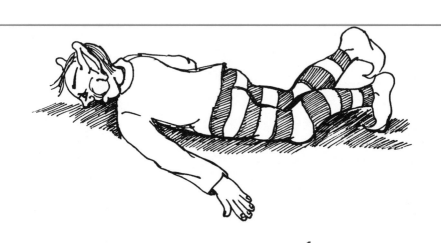

Prostrate—Prostate

Prostrate and *prostate* are two words that cause confusion for a lot of people, yet they are completely unrelated.

We become acquainted with *prostrate* early in life, usually in phys ed or gym class. It means "lying face down, prone," as in a position to do pushups. Also, one can become prostrate with exhaustion.

We hear more about *prostate* later in life. The prostate gland is a part of the male body. It frequently becomes cancerous in late life. Therefore, we hear and read many medical reports about prostate cancer.

One should learn the difference between these two similar words and be confident in his or her use of them.

Including the first r when pronouncing February is difficult.

February

February is notable as the shortest month, but it has another distinguishing feature. It is the only month whose pronunciation presents a problem.

The first *r* is frequently dropped, although sounding it is correct. But doing so makes the pronunciation more difficult.

What we most often hear is "Feb-u-ary," a pronunciation that very likely results from the close association with *January,* which does not have the first *r.*

Random House Dictionary says that although the pronunciation without the first *r* is sometimes criticized, it is used by educated speakers and is considered acceptable.

In reality, the pronunciations of both months most often sound like "Jan-yoo-wary" and "Feb-yoo-wary."

The ending of the word <u>asterisk</u> is not pronounced <u>rik</u>.

Asterisk

When pronouncing the word *asterisk,* many people tend to omit the second *s,* ending the word with *rik* rather than *risk.*

Such a pronunciation often results from the transposition of the last two letters, *s* and *k.* Some say *asterik* for the singular, *asteriks* for the plural.

This transposition is one of the reasons some say *aks* for *ask.*

Because the proper pronunciation of *asterisk* requires a little preciseness, some might feel that it comes across to others as affected or pretentious speech, when actually it is correct.

The ending of <u>poinsettia</u> can be pronounced <u>set-ah</u> or <u>set-ee-ah</u>.

Poinsettia

Is *poinsettia* pronounced *poin-set-ah* or *poin-set-ee-ah*? The question arises in the minds of many every Christmas season.

Both pronunciations are correct. It is just a matter of preference. (Incidentally, this popular Christmas plant is named for J. R. Poinsett, American minister to Mexico, who discovered it there in 1828.)

Is a Christmas tree *lighted* or *lit*? Both are correct and can be used in all contexts. However, in the adjective sense, *lighted* is probably more common, as in a *lighted* tree. But in the verb sense, *lit* probably gets the nod; for example, *he lit the tree.*

Roofs can be pronounced *rufs* or *rooves*.

Roofs—Rooves

When natural disasters such as hurricanes and floods are in the news, *roofs* are mentioned a lot, and we notice that the word is pronounced different ways—sometimes with the *f* sound, sometimes with the *v* sound, *ruvs.* Which is correct?

Many words that end in *f* require the *v* in pronunciation *and* spelling when converting to the plural (calf-calves, hoof-hooves, wolf-wolves), but *roof* is different.

Webster's Ninth New Collegiate Dictionary lists *roofs* and gives the pronunciation as *rufs.* But then it says "also ruvs," listing the latter only as a pronunciation option, not a spelling option.

At least two dictionaries show *rooves* as an optional spelling, but in one of them this version is identified as "disputed."

Random House Dictionary does not give the *v* version at all. It lists only *roofs* as the pronunciation and spelling.

Similar should not be pronounced *sim-u-lar*.

Similar

Confusion over the *uh* sound and the *yoo* sound sometimes causes some people to mispronounce *similar* and *manufacture.*

We frequently hear the *yoo* sound in the middle of *similar—simular—*when it should be the *uh* sound.

Yet, many of these same people will choose not to use the *yoo* sound when they should in the pronunciation of *manufacture,* which we hear as *manafacture.*

A related error occurs in the pronunciation of *confidentiality,* which is sometimes heard pronounced *confidenuality,* a *yoo* sound erroneously replacing the *che* sound for the *tia* syllable.

The same thing occurs with *unsubstantiated,* often heard as *unsubstanuated.*

Emphasis on the last syllable of some words

results in distorted pronunciations.

Distorted Pronunciations

The presidential campaign in 1992 gave national prominence to a pronunciation phenomenon that baffles most and annoys some. When did the pronunciation of *Clinton* change to *ClinTON,* with a little extra emphasis being placed on the second syllable?

The same could be asked of *hunter,* which, on a television show of the same name a few years ago, we repeatedly heard pronounced as *hunTER.* And we hear *menTAL, counTY, cenTER, AtlanTA,* and others.

These are slightly distorted pronunciations, and they seem to be contagious. Often those who hear them are not certain which way is proper.

One cannot say these pronunciations are wrong, but why they occur certainly is puzzling.

A thought or an opinion is an <u>idea</u>, not an <u>ideal</u>.

Idea—Ideal

Have you ever wondered why so many people use *ideal* when they mean *idea*? For example, "That's a good ideal" instead of *idea*.

An idea is a thought or an opinion, as in "I have an excellent idea to suggest to her." An ideal is a standard of excellence or a model to follow, as Johnny Carson is the ideal of many comedians.

Ideal and *idea* appear one after the other in the dictionary, but the meanings of the two are far apart in everyday usage.

Do not place an extra syllable where it is unnecessary.

Extra Syllable

There are a few words that some people like to add a syllable to for some strange reason. Two of them are *athlete* and *arthritis*. We often hear these pronounced *ath-a-lete* and *arth-a-ritis*. The middle syllable is entirely unnecessary and incorrect.

The word *veteran* is unusual in this sense. It has two acceptable pronunciations, *vet-er-ran* and *vet-tran,* listed in this order in most dictionaries, and one is about as popular as the other. So, here's an instance in which the extra syllable is actually acceptable, but which many choose not to use, very likely many of those same people who add the extra syllable to *athlete* and *arthritis*.

Isn't is pronounced by many as idn't.

Isn't—Idn't

Sometimes certain pronunciations develop because of things we aren't even aware of. Think about the terms *idn't* for *isn't* and *wudn't* for *wasn't*. These are widely used and are heard at all social levels.

In the process of forming one's mouth to speak these terms, the tip of the tongue, in anticipation of the *n* sound, touches the upper ridge of the mouth at the gum line and skips past the *s* sound, according to *Random House Dictionary of the English Language.*

Although it's not heard as often, the same thing occurs with those who pronounce *business* as *bidness.*

Many people incorrectly pronounce <u>didn't</u> as <u>ditn't</u>.

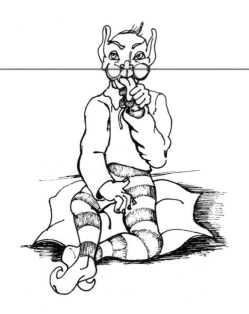

Didn't

Have you ever wondered why so many people pronounce the term *didn't* as if it were spelled *ditn't* (with a *t* in the middle instead of a *d*)?

This term is a combination of two words—*did* and *not.* We don't say *dit* for *did,* so why say *ditn't?* We hear the same thing happening with *wouldn't* and *couldn't* (a *t* sound replacing the *d* sound).

It's interesting to note that few (if any) incorrectly use a *t* instead of the *d* when writing these terms, even those who mispronounce them.

It is incorrect to pronounce a <u>th</u> sound
on the end of <u>height</u>.

Height

A strange thing about the word *height* is the way many people pronounce it as *heighth,* with a *th* sound on the end. It is heard about as often one way as it is the other. But *height*—it rhymes with *fight*—is the standard or correct version.

Consider it this way: *Weight,* which has the same kind of ending as *height,* is never heard pronounced with a *th* sound on the end. Carrying it one step further, it's *height-en* (sounds like *hite-en*) instead of *height-thin* when referring to making something higher.

The l in salmon is silent.

Salmon

Some words are tricky to pronounce just because of the way they look. When you order salmon at a restaurant or supermarket, do you pronounce the *l*? If so, you are wrong. It is spelled *salmon* but is pronounced as if it were spelled *sammon*. The *l* is silent.

A word that is becoming more and more bothersome for some to spell is *extension*. We see it spelled frequently with a *t* replacing the *s*. Oddly enough, since the ending *tion* sounds just like the *sion* ending, *extention* looks and sounds correct, but isn't. *Extension* is the correct version.

Momento is often confused with memento.

Momento—Memento

Did you hold on to a memento—a souvenir—from your last big vacation trip? Or is it *momento*? You hear it both ways. *Memento* is sometimes spelled and pronounced with the *mo* sound.

The word actually comes from the term *remember.* Therefore, *memento* is correct, but *momento* is seen and heard so often today that some authorities on words consider it merely a variant rather than a misuse of the word.

Often is more often pronounced off-en,

without a t sound.

Often

You've heard it pronounced *off-ten* and *off-en,* and chances are, you've wondered which is correct. According to *Random House Dictionary of the English Language, often* was pronounced with the *t* sound—*off-ten*—until the 17th century, when a pronunciation without the *t* sound became popular with the educated.

That's when the *t* sound fell into disfavor and the pronunciation became *off-en.* But the pronunciation with the *t* sound is so commonly used today that it has regained some of its standing. Now, both pronunciations are accepted, but *off-en* has a slight edge.

Affect means to influence; *effect* means a result.

Affect—Effect

Affect and *effect* will cause many people to pause before using one of them, and still the writer often chooses the wrong one.

In everyday language, *affect* means to influence. Example: His drinking affected his driving.

Effect means a result. Example: The effect of it all was that we won the game.

Effect can also be used as a verb, but such usage is not common with most people. An example: She will effect a lot of changes when she takes over.

Accept and *except* are also often confused with each other.

Accept means to receive, as in *accept a gift*. *Except* means to leave out, as in "They all went except John."

In behalf of and *on behalf of* are interchangeable.

In Behalf—On Behalf

Is it *in behalf of* or *on behalf of*?

Many people who use one of these phrases often are not sure whether their choice—*in* or *on*—is correct.

Actually, neither one is wrong. The two phrases may be and are used interchangeably.

Some usage authorities say *on behalf of* means "as the agent or representative of." Example: Your spouse is absent and you act on behalf of him or her.

These authorities further say that *in behalf of* means "in support of." Example: The witness testified in behalf of the defendant.

The American Heritage Dictionary, Third Edition, says: "The two senses are quite close, however, and are often confused, even by reputable writers."

The use of <u>ahold</u> for <u>hold</u> is widespread.

Get Ahold Of

"I was able to get ahold of . . ." the Chicago caller began. "Ahold. That's bad grammar, isn't it?" he interjected, questioning his use.

"Not really," I answered.

Several dictionaries list *ahold* as being regional, but *Webster's Dictionary of English Usage* says if it is regional, "it is well spread around." The book lists evidence of the use of *ahold* in 17 states all across the country.

Ahold most often is preceded by *get* and similar words, such as *catch* and *take,* and is usually followed by *of,* as in the first sentence of this example.

Ahold is used more in speech than in writing.

Pour is sometimes mistakenly used for *pore*.

Pour—Pore

It seems that there should not be any confusion between the verbs *pour* and *pore,* but there is, according to a reader who says he often sees the wrong one used.

Pour—to cause to flow in a stream—is a more day-to-day word for most people than is *pore,* which means "to read or study carefully."

Therefore, some just naturally choose the *pour* spelling even in those instances in which *pore* should be the choice.

Pore is usually followed by *over.* Example: "He will pore over the problem tonight."

Sometimes it is followed by *on* or *through.* Examples: "She pored on the matter needlessly" and "Police pored through the debris looking for evidence."

'Tis and *'twas* are unusual contractions.

Xmas

'Tis the season . . . .

Christmas time brings with it a few words not often seen at other times of the year.

One of those words is the first word in this article, *'tis,* which is a contraction of *it is.*

Usually, the apostrophe that is inserted in a contraction to indicate a missing letter falls somewhere within the word. *'Tis* is bit unusual in that the missing letter is the first one, so that is where the apostrophe goes. The same rule applies to *'twas* for *it was.*

Another word of this season is *Xmas.* It has a long and respectable history, but the use of *Xmas* is criticized by some because it leaves *Christ* out of *Christmas.*

Xmas dates back to the 16th century. *X* is the first letter in the Greek spelling of *Christos,* which is *Christ.* Add *mas* and you have *Xmas,* which can be pronounced *kris-mas* or *ex-mas.*

A third word seen at this season is *O,* as in "O Christmas Tree." *O* is used in solemn or poetic language to lend earnestness to an appeal, according to *Random House Dictionary.*

SECTION 5

Trends affect clothing styles, but they also influence the way we say things and many words and terms we use. Vogue words are discussed in this section.

We hear these words and phrases, and suddenly it seems that everyone is using them.

Look on the following pages to see if there are some words and terms that you have made a part of your daily speech and writing.

Impacting and _networking_ are just two of the many vogue words that make their way into our vernacular.

Trendy Words

Much is written about clothing styles—what's vogue and the latest.

Little, however, is ever written or said about vogue words and terms, but they are very prevalent in our society.

A mystery about these expressions is how they spread so rapidly from one end of the continent to the other. A few examples are: *impacting; power* (as in power lunch and power vacation); and *networking* (as in sharing information).

Random House Dictionary says: "Vogue expressions demonstrate that their users are socially or professionally with it." But it adds: "Critics of vogue expressions are annoyed by the frequency with which these terms are used."

Speech habits are contagious.

In Harm's Way

On newscasts and in some news columns that tell of military strife in the world, someone is frequently reported either *in harm's way* or *out of harm's way.*

One or two people will use the phrase and soon every news anchor, columnist, and spokesperson is using it.

It is this sort of contagion that influences the grammar and punctuation usage of many people. They use what they hear and see others use, right or wrong, rarely looking in a book themselves.

Nothing is wrong with the *in harm's way* phrase, but its repeated use by so many clearly illustrates how people are quick to adopt the language habits of others. Unfortunately, they often are bad habits.

(The *in harm's way* quote is credited to John Paul Jones, an American naval hero 200 years ago, who said, "I wish to have no connection with any ship that does not sail fast; for I intend to go in harm's way.")

Dictionaries become dated.

Dated Dictionaries

Infrastructure. Is this word in your dictionary?

The presidential candidates tossed the word around freely in the 1992 campaign. Inquiries came in to the reference desks of libraries by people who couldn't find it in their dictionaries.

The word did not start appearing in dictionaries of general use until the 1960s, so these callers learned their dictionaries were dated.

It is said that the period of a person's college years can be established by looking at the date on his or her dictionary. If you have been out of school several years and haven't acquired a new dictionary since, perhaps you should consider doing so. Many new words and usages develop over the years. (Incidentally, a dictionary is an excellent gift.)

The American Heritage Dictionary, Third Edition, defines infrastructure as: "The basic facilities . . . needed for the functioning of a community or society, such as transportation and communications systems, water and power lines, and public institutions . . . ."

<u>How come</u> he never waits for us?

How Come—Why

"How come she chose that one?"

How come appears in dictionaries as a term meaning *why.* It is heard frequently.

The expression is informal, but authorities label it acceptable and useful in certain situations, even in writing.

Webster's Dictionary of English Usage says writers seem to find *how come* a stronger or more emphatic way to say *why.* Example: "How come he never waits for us?"

A similar term is *how so* meaning "how is it so?" An example from *American Heritage Dictionary, Third Edition,* is: "You say the answer is wrong. How so?"

Adding <u>ee</u> to words is common and widely accepted.

The ee Suffix

Is it proper to refer to a person designated to receive a copy of a letter as a *copyee*?

A reader used the word in a note to my column "Grammar Gremlins" and then halfway apologized for doing so, thinking it might be too informal, even in a note.

Adding the suffix *ee* to a verb to indicate the receiver of certain action is popular and widely accepted. Examples: *draftee, absentee, appointee, escapee,* and *attendee.*

The *ee* use showed up early in legal language—*trustee, lessee, grantee,* etc.—and later came into general use.

The *ee* suffix is often used in make-do words to fit a specific occasion, such as *copyee* in the note mentioned above, and especially in *er* and *ee* contrasts. Example: "When that romance ended, was she the droppee or the dropper?"

The use of the *ee* suffix has been around for generations, and its use is unlikely to change, because oftentimes it effectively expresses the thought. Many of its uses, though, remain informal.

Done seems to have become popular.

Done—Finished—Through

There has been much debate through the years about the use of *done* for *finished* and *through,* but for some strange reason, *done* seems to have taken over in recent times.

Credit this perhaps to our being copycats; we hear someone use a word or expression and then we start using it. Then others do, and suddenly it seems everyone is using it.

Instead of hearing, "They were finished with their meal" or "She was through with her project," we now quite often hear "They were done . . ." or "She was done . . . ."

Used in the sense to describe something, all three words—finished, through, done—are standard, but it seems that *done* has become the current favorite of many.

Butt is slang or at best, informal.

Butt

There are five entries for *butt* in most dictionaries, but this is not a recent development. It had the same number 75 years ago.

What *is* recent is the common use of the word in the *buttocks* sense in places and situations one would not expect to hear or see it used.

Butt in this sense is described as informal by some dictionaries and as slang by others. *Slang* has a variety of meanings, two of which are "speech or writing that is very informal" and "speech or writing that is socially taboo."

A reader suggested this article on *butt* because she noticed its frequent use almost everywhere. At about the same time, a female at a major mail-order house, in telling me in a very pleasant manner the company's delivery schedule, said liberal deadlines were quoted by the company "to cover its butt," meaning to allow ample time for deliveries.

A few words and sounds are common

as filler for pauses in speech.

Like—Go

A reader offered interesting comments about uses of *like* and *go* which make him cringe now but which he said he regularly used at a younger age.

His illustrations were: "Like, I saw this TV show . . ." and "So I go, 'listen, if you want . . . .' "

When used this way, *like* is filler, a term applied to words, phrases, and sounds that are used by many people in their speech to fill pauses. *Uh* and *you know* are two common fillers.

As for *go* meaning *say, Webster's Dictionary of English Usage* notes that this use first attracted the attention of language observers in the mid-1970s.

These observers say such uses of *like* and *go* are informal and characteristic of speech, not of writing.

Chairman is still an acceptable term.

Chairman

In this day of gender awareness, the old reliable term *chairman* has come under a lot of scrutiny and is avoided by many.

The use of *chair* to refer to this leadership role is often criticized, but the term is quite acceptable.

In fact, *chair* and *chairman* in this sense both came along at about the same time, in the mid-1600s.

Chairwoman, which dates back to the late 1600s, is a natural companion to *chairman,* but it is "perceived as a less weighty word," says Rosalie Maggio in *The Bias-Free Word Finder.*

She notes that *chairperson* is awkward and seems to be used mostly for women.

The Associated Press Stylebook says: "Do not use *chairperson* unless it is an organization's formal title for an office." The AP specifies *chairman* or *chairwoman.*

Webster's Dictionary of English Usage says all four of these words "are in standard use, and you can use whichever you like best."

The plural <u>guys</u> may apply to both sexes.

Guys

"Can I get anything else for you guys?" the waitress asked of the foursome consisting of two women and two men.

Can this be right? Are women *guys*? Strangely enough, when used in the plural, *guys* can apply to members of a group of either sex or both sexes.

But in the singular, *guy* usually refers only to a male.

In her book *The Bias-Free Word Finder,* Rosalie Maggio says: "*Guy* seems here to stay even though its companion term *gal* would rarely be appropriate in similar situations."

She adds, "When used colloquially, the plural *guys* has become acceptable for both sexes."

On a related subject, author Maggio says *pal* is more often used of boys and men "but is also correctly used of girls and women."

SECTION 6

Who sets the rules? Who tells you what to say, how to say it, and what punctuation to use?

Is it really important that you use proper grammar and punctuation? Who notices?

How does one resolve the nagging questions that arise as he or she is trying to compose a letter or memorandum?

You are more or less on your own. The challenge is yours.

The Challenge

There are no laws of grammar that you must obey, only rules. If you park your automobile in a no-parking zone and receive a parking ticket, you *know* you have done something wrong. The ticket tells you so.

If you get a speeding ticket and have to go to court because of it, you really get the message that you have done something wrong. But if you use poor grammar in pleading your case, the judge is not going to say, "You made four grammatical errors in your testimony. Your fine is fifty dollars higher."

Heaven forbid! You wouldn't tell someone he made a grammatical error. It is a difficult thing to do. Why is this? We do not hesitate to correct a person's arithmetic errors.

If a cashier, when counting out your change to you, makes a mistake and shortchanges you two dollars, you will tell him or her about it. But if that cashier uses poor grammar in discussing the transaction, you would say nothing about the grammar. You would not say to the clerk: "By the way, you need to work on your agreement of subject and verb and on your verb tenses."

We can only imagine what would happen. The clerk would be insulted, yet that same clerk would very likely apologize for shortchanging you and immediately correct the mistake.

Our use of the English language is one of the key standards by which we are measured socially, professionally, and academically, but many Americans seem to be losing the ability to use proper grammar. It is almost as if few care anymore.

Washington Post columnist William Raspberry once wrote that the "proper use of the language is routinely accepted as a mark of intelligence, the first basis on which we are judged by those whose judgments matter.

"You may be quite a decent computer programmer," he said, "but few prospective employers will believe it if you speak poorly. You may have the skills necessary to become a first-rate manager, but if you can't write a decent memo . . . you are likely to be thought incompetent.

"We regularly make judgments as to the brightness, the competency, and the intelligence of people we meet—not by giving them examinations in their specialties but by observing how they use the language," Raspberry wrote.

The message here is, if one speaks properly, we assume that that person has some degree of intelligence, but if he or she uses poor grammar, we think just the opposite. Think back on it; you have made early judgments about others just by hearing or seeing the grammar they used.

I recall seeing two members of the Hell's Angels motorcycle group being interviewed on the television show "60 Minutes" and noted how properly they spoke. They used very good grammar—grammar that could easily have led viewers to think they were watching college professors or bank presidents. My opinion of the two rose just a little bit as I watched and listened to them speak. I was impressed. I momentarily overlooked that they were members of a questionable group.

A high school teacher once told me that in some instances students who use proper grammar are criticized by their peers as trying to be "hifalutin" or too "la-di-da." Male students in particular sometimes try to avoid speaking properly, fearing they will sound prissy, the teacher said.

A New York advertising executive wrote in *Advertising Age* on the poor use of grammar: "It's not just the kids and the underprivileged that are committing these grammar crimes; it's the better-educated among us, the teachers, the journalists, my business associates, my friends. Don't these people hear what they are saying?" We might also ask, "Don't they read what they are writing?"

If you intend to be accurate in your use of grammar, you will have to have a couple of reference books handy so you can look up those points about which you are in doubt. But merely having the reference books available is not enough; you must take time to use them.

If you are writing something and have a question, you must stop and look up the point right then. If you do not take the moment at that time to do so, you will have the same question again. In our rushed society, it is sometimes difficult to slow down long enough to look in a grammar or usage book, but doing so is the only way you will ever resolve those nagging little grammar questions you encounter.

As you make more frequent use of the reference books, you will become more skilled at using them, and you will be able to find your answers quickly. It is just like typing; the more you do it, the better you get.

Another good thing to do is make a note when you see or hear a point you question, and then look it up later if it is not convenient to do so at the time. Jot down a short note—maybe it will be just a two-word reminder—or you will not remember the point you wanted to research.

The chances are that you do not have a problem with many points of grammar, usage, or punctuation, maybe only a very few. What you should do is concentrate on those that give you the most trouble and resolve them. After you tuck those away in your memory, branch out a little bit to other troublesome points. Do not try to resolve all your grammar problems at once.

It is your challenge to know when to watch your p's and q's of grammar. Obviously, if you are trying to win a big contract in a business transaction, or if you are writing a report for your department manager, or a cover letter for your résumé, you should take care to express yourself more accurately and properly than you would in, for instance, a letter to your sister. But even your sister would probably appreciate a well-constructed and properly phrased and properly punctuated letter.

What about the last thank-you note you wrote? Were you comfortable with the way it read? What about the last one you received? Did it contain any errors in grammar, usage, or punctuation?

The most profound words lose their impact if they are conveyed in a speech, a letter, or a report that contains grammatical errors. Wherever you say it or write it, poor grammar and incorrect or omitted punctuation will reveal your shortcomings.

Please remember, just because someone is not pointing out your errors to you does not mean he or she has not seen or heard the errors. People will not tell you about these mistakes. Therefore, you are more or less on your own to detect your mistakes in grammar, usage, and punctuation and to correct them.

INDEX